D0487084

For my parents Lyn and Erich

Many thanks to the staff and children at
Flamingo Montessori Day Nursery, Burnham, Berkshire
and Teeny Boppers Nursery, Slough, Berkshire
for their help and advice.

Copyright © 1996 De Agostini Editions Ltd
Illustrations copyright © 1996 Paul Hess

Edited by Anna McQuinn and Ambreen Husain, designed by Sarah Godwin and Suzy McGrath

While every effort has been made to trace the present copyright holders
we apologise in advance for any unintentional omission or error and will
be pleased to insert the appropriate acknowledgment in any subsequent edition.
Grateful acknowledgment is made to the following for permission to reprint the material listed below:
Monkey copyright © 1996 Miles Gibson.
The Parrot by Zarina Husain, copyright © 1998 Zero to Ten Ltd.
Aardvark and **Jaguar** from The ABC of Bumptious Beasts by Gail Kredenser,
copyright © 1966 Gail Kredenser, reprinted by permission of Gail Kredenser Mack.
The Snake and **Toucans Two** copyright © 1983 by Jack Prelutsky from Zoo Doings, 1983,
reprinted by permission of Greenwillow Books (a division of William Morrow & Company, Inc.).
The Tapir copyright © 1996 Carol Pike.
The Tree Frog copyright © John Travers Moore from Cinnamon Seed.

First published in Great Britain in 1996 by De Agostini Editions.
First paperback edition published in 1998 by Zero to Ten Ltd., 46 Chalvey Road East Slough, Berkshire, SL1 2LR.

All rights reserved.

No part of the publication may be reproduced or utilized in any form or by any means,
electronic or mechanical, including photocopying, recording or by any information retrieval system,
without the prior written permission of the Publishers.

A CIP catalogue record for this book is available from the British Library.

ISBN 1-84089 040-1

Printed and bound in Spain.

Rainforest Animals

Illustrated by

PAUL HESS

COUNTY
LIBRARY

Monkey

IF YOU WANT to catch a monkey
You're guaranteed to fail
Until you learn to leap from trees
While swinging by your tail.

Parrot

PURPLE, green, red, blue or yellow
The parrot is a colourful fellow
He sits at the top of a tropical tree
And loudly squawks – "Hey, look at me!"

Anteater

THE ANTEATER'S a nosy beast
With a sniffley, snuffley snoot;
He comes out at night for his evening feast,
A shuffling, whuffling brute.

Snake

DON'T ever make the bad mistake
of stepping on the sleeping snake
because his jaws
might be awake.

Jaguar

THE JAGUAR is wild – she's a jungle cat
With a frightfully loud sort of purr.
Her fine spotted coat
Gives her reason to gloat
And to spend the day licking her fur.

Toucan

WHATEVER one toucan can do
is sooner done by toucans two,
and three toucans (it's very true)
can do much more than two can do.

Tapir

THE TAPIR has no manners,
He picks food with his nose.
He swims and stomps the moonlit swamps,
With stubby little toes.

Tree Frog

"DEE DEEP," he says
And stops, till when
It's time to say
"Dee deep" again.